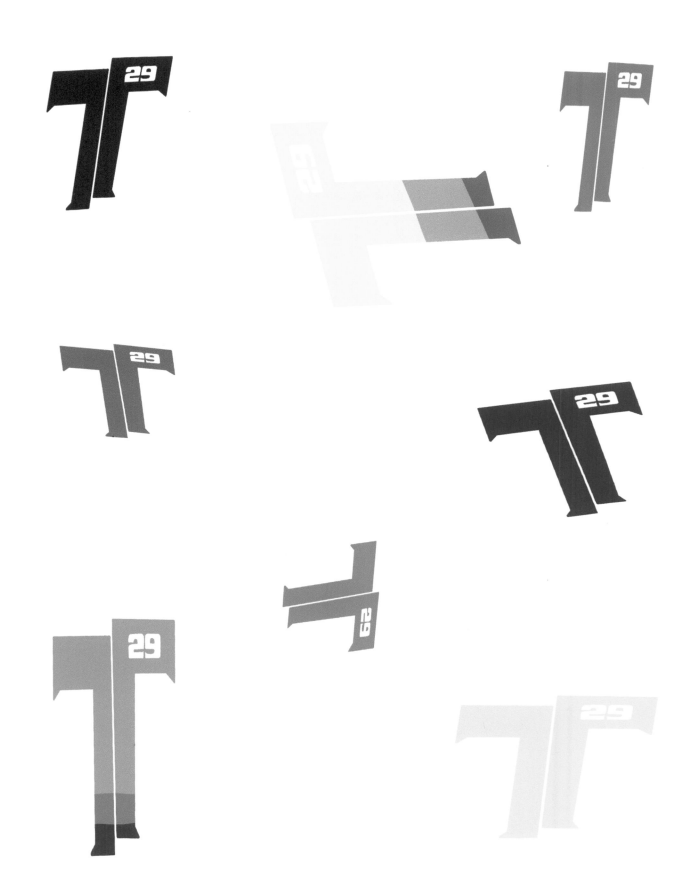

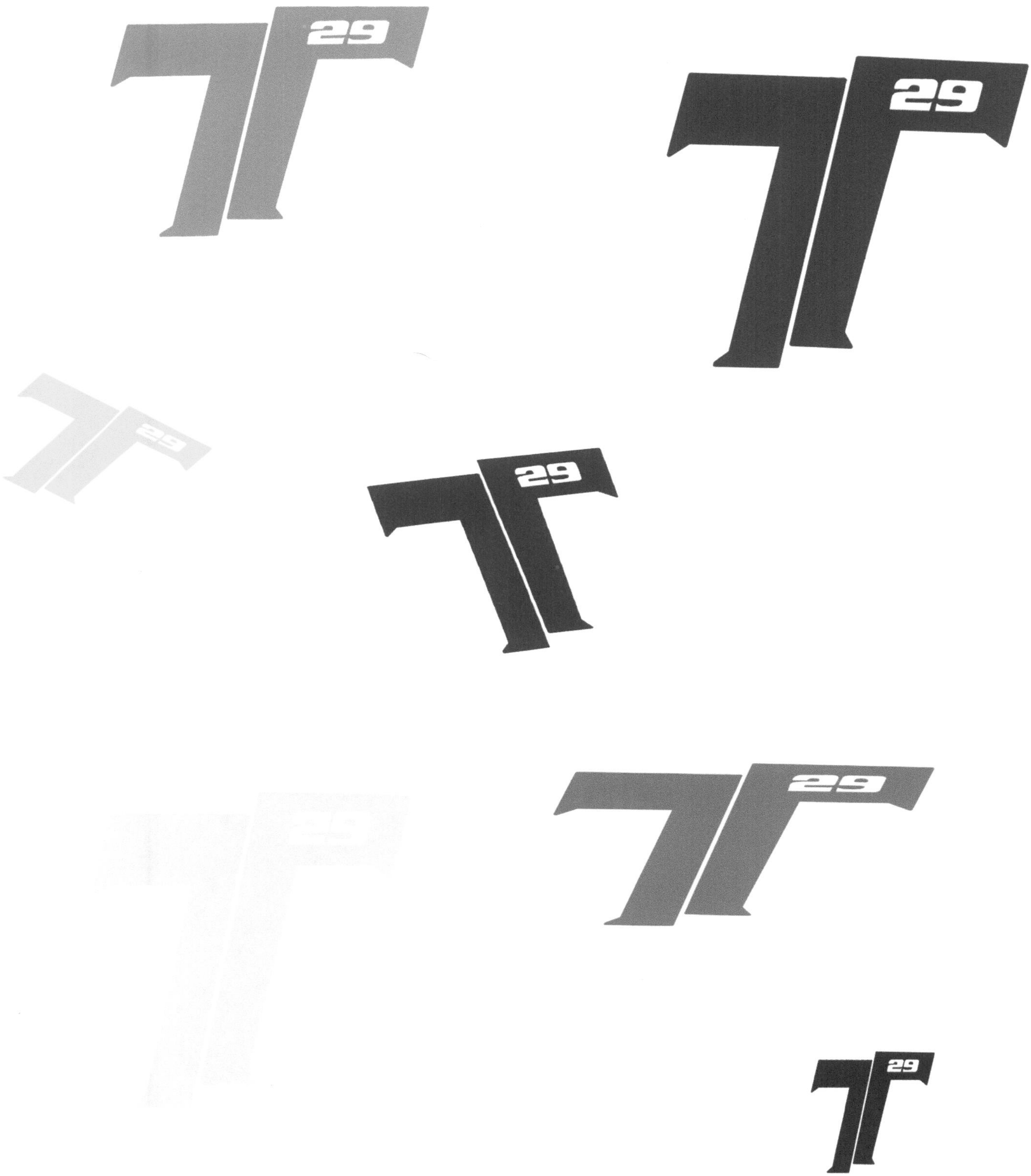
29

To my son Tyler Fyfe Downey

TYLER TRAVELS
NEW YORK CITY

Written by Lucius Downey

Illustrated by LaMont Russ

Tyler always wanted to travel, and one of the first places he wanted to visit was New York City—the city that never sleeps.

He was amazed at all the different buildings—big, tall, short, and small.

First stop, the Empire State Building—one of the tallest buildings in
New York City. Tyler was excited. He took the elevator to the highest
floor. "Look, Dad! It's the observation deck!" Tyler circled the entire
deck overlooking the city.

"I can see the Statue of Liberty," Tyler shouted.
He was so excited he pointed with his finger and started smiling.
"Daddy, can that be our next stop please, pretty please?"

Tyler and his parents took a ferry from Battery Park to Liberty Island to see the Statue of Liberty. Wowed by the statue's height and size, Tyler just couldn't stop looking up.
"Mom, I can't believe how tall she is," he said.

Off the ferry and back on dry land, they stopped by a place where everyone from around the world comes to visit: Times Square. Tyler was mesmerized by the bright lights that can be seen from outer space, along with all the huge TV screens on the buildings. Suddenly he froze, and he smelled something familiar, something delicious like fresh from the oven.

He followed the smell to the famous Joe's Pizza.
With a slice in hand, cheese, and pepperoni dripping,
Tyler couldn't believe how yummy it was.
"Best pizza ever!" he shouted.

With Tyler's tummy full, he's ready to hop on the train for the first time. "Zoom zoom, off to Central Park we go," he yelled at the top of his lungs.

After staring at the park map for a few seconds, with happiness, he whispered to himself. "Look at all of those people riding bikes!" Tyler loves bicycles, so he and his parents rode around the park. With kites flying and birds chirping, they rode through trails, passed by ponds and churned over hills, which led them to a place Tyler didn't know existed.

Jumping joyously in his father's arms, he could not believe he was at the Central Park Zoo. "Look, Mom! Look, Dad!

Who said bears can't live in the city," Tyler said jokingly.

The sun started setting and it was time to leave. Tyler yawned and appeared to be drifting off during the train ride. He's tired, but not tired of traveling, and is already thinking of his next adventure.

Hmmm... Where do you think he will go next?

TYLER

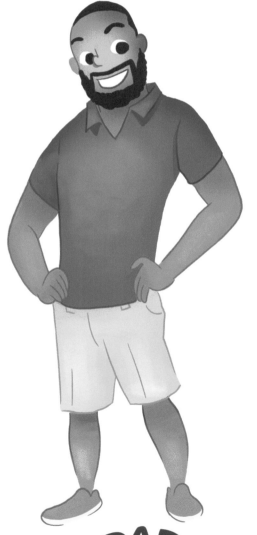

DAD

MOM

I ♥ NY

THE BIG APPLE

TIMES SQ

MADISON AVE

SUBWAY

5

Tyler Travels - New York City by Lucius Downey

Published by Lucius Downey

New Britain, CT 06051

www.TylerClub29.com

Illustrations by Lamont Russ

ISBN: 978-1-7378790-0-8

Library of Congress Control Number: 2021918178

Printed in the U.S.A

First Edition

Can you find ALL of the hidden "T's?"

PLEASE LiKE, SHARE, AND FOLLOW. TO PURCHASE MERCHANDiSE AND DOWNLOAD FUN ACTiViTiES ViSiT TYLERCLUB29.COM

TYLERCLUB29.COM

@TYLERCLUB29

@TYLERCLUB29

CPSIA information can be obtained
at www.ICGtesting.com
Printed in the USA
LVHW070925020822
724968LV00008B/59